Why People Should Visit Uluru

Carmel Reilly

Contents

A Special Place

Uluru is an enormous rock in the desert
in the middle of Australia.

It is home to the **Anangu** people.
They have lived there for thousands of years.
It is also home to many **native** animals and plants.

I feel that everyone should visit Uluru,
to learn about this important part of Australia
and the people who have lived there for so long.

Uluru is in the Northern Territory in Australia.

A Wonderful Rock

I think that Uluru is really wonderful to look at.
It is so large that it can be seen
from a long way away across the desert.

Visitors love to take photos of this huge rock,
because it is such an amazing sight.

When the sun rises in the morning,
the colour of Uluru can turn from brown to orange.

In the evening, as the sun goes down over the desert,
the rock can seem to be a deep red colour,
and then it quickly turns to purple.

Uluru can look purple in the evening.

Uluru can seem to be a deep red colour.

Lots to Do and See

There is a lot to do and see at Uluru. There are tracks for people to walk along, and springs, waterholes and caves to visit.

Many birds, **reptiles** and other animals, such as kangaroos, live near the rock and in the desert close by. More than 400 kinds of native plants can be found there, as well.

Many types of lizards can be found near Uluru.

The Anangu People

I feel that visiting Uluru is a very good way to learn about and meet the Anangu people. The Anangu people have lived near Uluru for thousands of years.

This huge rock and many of the places close by are very special to them.

When visitors go to Uluru,
they are taken around the rock by Anangu **guides**.
The guides tell the visitors stories about Uluru
and about the Anangu people.
They talk about their art and their music, too.

Living in the Desert

At Uluru, Anangu guides talk to visitors
about how their people
have been able to live in the desert for so long.
They talk about the long distances
they have to walk sometimes to find food and water.
They show the visitors
how to find and cook bush food, as well.

Protecting the Rock

The guides tell visitors about their laws.
Uluru is such an important place,
and the Anangu people
have very strong feelings about it.
Their laws help the Anangu people
care for each other and their land.

Visitors are asked not to climb on the rock.
The Anangu people want to protect it.
They want to keep people safe, too,
because the rock is so high and slippery.

There is so much to do and learn at Uluru.
I feel that everyone should visit
this beautiful part of Australia.

'We Don't Climb'

'That's a really important sacred thing that you are climbing...

You shouldn't climb. It's not the real thing about this place.

The real thing is listening to everything. This is the thing that's right.

This is the proper way: no climbing.'

© **Kunmanara**
Traditional Owner

Please Don't Climb Uluṟu

Our traditional Law teaches us the proper way to behave. We ask you to respect our Law by not climbing Uluṟu.

What visitors call 'the climb' is the traditional route taken by ancestral Mala men upon their arrival at Uluṟu in the creation time. It has great spiritual significance.

We have a responsibility to teach and safeguard visitors to our land. 'The climb' is dangerous and too many people have died while attempting to climb Uluṟu. Many others have been injured while climbing. We feel great sadness when a person dies or is hurt on our land. We worry about you and we worry about your family.

Glossary

Anangu *(proper noun)*	Aboriginal people who have lived close to Uluru for thousands of years
guides *(noun)*	people who show visitors around a place
native *(adjective)*	describes plants and animals that belong to an area
reptiles *(noun)*	animals, such as snakes and lizards, that have cold blood